Father-Son Connection

Written and Illustrated by
Jonathan Hill

Copyright 2023 Jonathan Hill
ISBN: 978-1-961443-12-9
All Rights Reserved. No part of this book may
be reproduced in any form without permission
in writing from the publisher.
All inquires about this book can be
sent to the author at info@harbourhousepress.co.uk

Get Free Color by Number book send a Mail
After Purchase to info@harbourhousepress.co.uk

Dedicated to my Kids:
Val, Vishal and Videl

HOUSE PUBLISHING LTD

When the world feels like an overwhelming maze, I'll hold your hand tightly, leading you through the darkest corners, illuminating the way with love and unwavering guidance.

As you face the challenges of the world, my son, know that I will stand as your unwavering protector, shielding you from adversity, and empowering you with the belief that you possess the strength and resilience to overcome any obstacle.

In moments of vulnerability and tears, my arms will be your shelter, offering solace and a safe space to find comfort and reassurance.

When challenges test your spirit, I'll stand beside you, an unwavering pillar of strength, reminding you of the untapped reservoir of courage and resilience within your soul.

With each step you take towards your dreams, I'll be your loudest cheerleader, witnessing your triumphs with tears of pride, knowing that your success is a testament to your boundless potential.

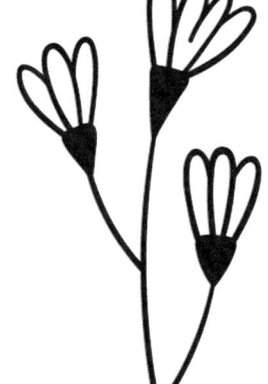

When life becomes an exhausting whirlwind, we'll escape together, forging unforgettable memories, as I show you the beauty that exists in the simplest moments, reminding you of the infinite wonder in the world.

In times of self-doubt, I'll be your unwavering mirror of truth, reflecting back the extraordinary person you are, showering you with reminders of your inherent worth and the incredible impact you make.

As you embark on your life's journey, my son, know that I will always walk beside you, unwavering in my support and love, proud to be your dad, and forever grateful for the extraordinary bond we share.

When you seek guidance and inspiration, my son, I will be your unwavering compass, illuminating your path with wisdom, encouraging you to embrace your passions, and reminding you of the incredible potential that resides within you.

In moments of solitude or uncertainty, remember, my son, that you are never alone. I am here, a constant presence in your life, ready to listen, understand, and provide the comfort and reassurance that only a father can offer.

As you face the challenges of the world, my son, know that I will stand as your unwavering protector, shielding you from adversity, and empowering you with the belief that you possess the strength and resilience to overcome any obstacle.

When life presents its complexities, my son, turn to me, your trusted advisor, sharing the knowledge and lessons I've learned, helping you navigate the twists and turns with grace and confidence.

In times of uncertainty or self-doubt, my son, lean on me, your unwavering pillar of strength. Believe in yourself, for you are capable of achieving greatness. I will always encourage you to pursue your dreams with unwavering determination.

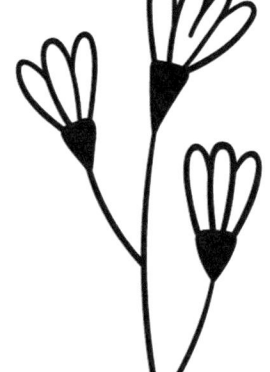

When you yearn for connection and embrace, my son, know that my arms are always open wide, ready to envelop you in a warm embrace, offering solace, love, and the reassurance that you are cherished beyond measure.

In moments of discouragement, my son, remember that you are destined for greatness. I will be your biggest cheerleader, igniting the fire within you, reminding you of your resilience, and urging you to never lose sight of your limitless potential.

Together, my son, let us embark on thrilling adventures, creating memories that will last a lifetime. I will be your partner-in-crime, your confidant, and your biggest fan, ensuring that we seize every precious moment with joy and laughter.

www.ingramcontent.com/pod-product-compliance
Lightning Source LLC
Chambersburg PA
CBRC091204010526
44107CB00021B/1242